DESIGN THE LIFE YOU DESERVE

A TRANSFORMATIVE 12-WEEK JOURNEY FOR STUDENTS

SIMBLE T ASHOKAN

To my son Ivaan and my daughter Ivaaniya,

You are the light of my life and my greatest inspiration. Your love, care, and unwavering belief in me give me strength every single day. Through your laughter and innocence, you remind me of the beauty of life and the power of dreams.

To the students who feel stuck, overwhelmed, or uncertain about their future,

This book is a guiding light for you to design the life you deserve.

May you all find the courage to dream big,

The strength to overcome challenges,

And the wisdom to create a life filled with purpose and joy.

Contents

PREFACE

Dear Students,

Growing up, I was always a good student, earning high marks and receiving praise for my academic performance. However, despite my achievements, I had no clear idea about what I truly wanted to do with my life. My grades were strong, so I chose engineering, a path that seemed logical at the time. I completed my M.E. in Computer Science and Engineering, but deep down, I knew it wasn't the right fit for me.

After working at Federal Bank and as an Assistant Professor in an Engineering College, I decided to pursue a new direction in life. I followed my true calling and shifted my career towards life coaching. Alongside this, I completed my M.A. in Psychology with a focus on counseling, which provided me with deeper insights into human behavior and personal development.

Looking back, I often wonder: if I had known earlier what field truly suited me, how much more could I have achieved? I believe that understanding our passions and strengths at a young age can pave the way for greater success and fulfillment. However, like many others, I faced personal challenges along the way that I didn't know how to solve at the time. These challenges made me realize the importance of not just academic success, but also the ability to face difficulties head-on and make decisions that align with our true values and goals.

In school and colleges, we are often not taught how to handle obstacles, how to make decisions with confidence, or how to build financial freedom, maintain friendships, or achieve peace and happiness. We learn how to excel in subjects but not how to live a fulfilling and balanced life. These are the lessons I wish I had understood earlier.

As a life coach, consultant psychologist, author, and YouTuber, I now work with individuals to help them navigate their challenges, make informed decisions, and create meaningful lives. This book is my attempt to share the knowledge I've gathered, to help you face life's challenges, make empowering decisions, and build a life that brings peace, joy, and success.

With all my love & support,
Simble T ashokan

ACKNOWLEDGEMENTS

This book has been a journey of passion, perseverance, and purpose, and I am deeply grateful to all who have supported and inspired me along the way.

First and foremost, **I thank God** for being my guiding light and strength through every step of this journey. Without His blessings, none of this would have been possible.

To my family—my father, **Ashokan Thaipparambil,** and my mother, **Kanakalatha**—your unwavering love and encouragement have been my foundation.

To my beloved children, **Ivaan and Ivaaniya**, you are my heart and soul. Your smiles and love are my greatest motivation.

To my sister's daughters, **Avinbala and Krishnabala**, your youthful energy and curiosity remind me to always embrace life with wonder.

To my cherished friends, **RoseRani,Shabeena A M, Minu Anna Mathew, and Deena**, thank you for being my constant cheerleaders and for believing in me, even when I doubted myself.

To **my teachers at HMYSHS School,** your guidance and wisdom shaped the person I am today. I am forever grateful for the values and knowledge you instilled in me.

To my clients—words cannot express my deep gratitude to each of you. Your trust in me and your journeys of growth and transformation have been my greatest inspiration. You have taught me so much, and I feel honored to have been part of your stories.

To myself—thank you for believing in your vision, staying persistent through challenges, and embracing growth. This is a reminder that self-belief and determination can create wonders.

To my mentors, supporters, and every reader holding this book, this journey would not have been possible without you. I hope this book inspires you to design a life that is meaningful and fulfilling.

With heartfelt gratitude,
Simble
Mobile: +91 8281556616

Prologue

We all dream of a life that is fulfilling, meaningful, and uniquely ours—a life that resonates with our deepest desires and aspirations. Yet, as students, life often feels like a whirlwind of expectations, deadlines, and choices. We are told to dream big but are rarely guided on how to turn those dreams into reality.

This book is your guide, your companion on a transformative 12-week journey to design the life you truly deserve. It is not just about theories or lofty ideas but about practical steps, actionable strategies, and thought-provoking exercises that empower you to take charge of your life.

Over the course of these chapters, we will explore the foundations of self-awareness, the courage to overcome fears, the art of mastering time, and the power of building meaningful relationships. You will discover how to create a perfect daily routine, set goals that inspire you, and take actions that align with your dreams.

This book is more than a guide; it is a call to action. It is an invitation to reflect, learn, and grow. Each chapter is designed to inspire you, challenge you, and equip you with the tools you need to navigate life's complexities with confidence and clarity.

As you turn these pages, remember that this journey is yours. **Bring your pen, your notebook, and your willingness to embrace change.** Reflect deeply, participate wholeheartedly, and apply these lessons to your life.

Together, let's unlock your potential, chart your path, and design a life that is truly yours—a life that is purposeful, joyful, and extraordinary.

Welcome to the journey of transformation.

With love and encouragement,
Simble
+91 8281556616

I

Week 1 – Know Yourself: Self-Discovery & Self-Awareness

Welcome!

Are you ready to start a journey of transformation? This week is all about **YOU**—understanding your strengths, values, and interests. **Grab a notebook and pen,** and dedicate this book to your journey. Make it your personal guide and a place to reflect, plan, and grow.

Let's dive into knowing yourself better—it's going to be fun, interactive, and deeply rewarding!

The Power of Self-Awareness

Self-awareness is the ability to recognize and understand your emotions, strengths, weaknesses, values, and desires. **It's about truly knowing who you are**, what motivates you, and what brings you fulfillment. Developing self-awareness is the first step toward designing a life that's in alignment with your true self.

When you are self-aware, you make better decisions, build stronger relationships, and lead a more meaningful life. It helps you understand your passions, identify your strengths, and acknowledge areas that need growth. In short, self-awareness is the key to unlocking your potential and creating the life you've always dreamed of.

This week, we're going to begin uncovering your true self. You'll gain insight into your strengths, core values, and interests—things that will guide your actions and decisions as you work toward your goals

Why Knowing Yourself Matters

Before you plan where to go, you must know where you're starting. This week, we'll:

- Identify your strengths and areas of improvement.
- Explore what truly matters to you (your core values).
- Discover your passions and interests.
- Reflect on past successes to build confidence.

Each exercise will help you uncover new insights about yourself and set the stage for designing your dream life.

Exercise 1: SWOT Analysis

Time Required: 20 minutes

In your notebook, divide a page into four sections and label them: Strengths, Weaknesses, Opportunities, and Threats. Now, answer the following questions:

1. **Strengths**

- What are you naturally good at?
- What skills have others complimented you on?
- What makes you feel proud or confident?

2. **Weaknesses**

- What tasks or skills do you find challenging?
- Are there any habits holding you back?
- What feedback do you often receive from others?

3. **Opportunities**

What resources or relationships can help you grow?

- Are there opportunities you've been ignoring?
- What new skills or experiences can you explore?

4. **Threats**

- What obstacles or fears are blocking your progress?
- Are there any distractions or time-wasters in your life?

Action Step:
Write 1–2 action points for each category to either build on your strengths or address weaknesses, opportunities, and threats.

Exercise 2: Discover Your Core Values

Time Required: 15 minutes
Your core values guide every decision you make. Understanding them will help you design a life aligned with your true self.
Instructions
Write down answers to these prompts:

- What qualities do you admire in others?
- When do you feel the most fulfilled and proud?
- What activities or causes light a fire in you?

Here's a list of values to inspire you

- Honesty
- Growth
- Freedom
- Kindness
- Adventure
- Creativity

Action Step
Choose your top 5 core values and write why each is important to you.

Exercise 3: Identify Your Interests

Time Required: 15 minutes

Discover what excites you! Your interests are clues to the career, hobbies, and goals that align with your passions.

Instructions

Answer these questions in your notebook:

- What topics make you lose track of time?
- What hobbies or skills have you always enjoyed?
- Is there something you've always wanted to learn but haven't yet?

Action Step

- Make a list of 3 interests you want to explore this month.
- Schedule a time this week to learn about or try one of them.

Exercise 4: Reflect on Past Successes

Time Required: 10 minutes

Think about moments when you felt truly proud or accomplished. These memories remind you of your strengths and potential.

Instructions

Answer these prompts:

- What's a time when you overcame a challenge?
- What's your biggest achievement so far?
- What did you learn from these experiences?

Action Step

Write a short paragraph about how these successes reflect your strengths and potential.

Daily Reflection Habit

Each day this week, spend 5–10 minutes journaling about what you've discovered. Use these prompts to guide your reflection:

- What did I learn about myself today?
- What surprised me?
- How do I feel about this journey so far?

Checklist for the Week

By the end of this week, you should:

1. Complete your SWOT analysis.
2. Identify your top 5 core values.
3. List your top 3 interests and explore at least one.
4. Reflect on at least two past successes.

What Did You Learn?

At the end of the week, answer these reflection questions:

- What was the most powerful insight you gained?
- How do you feel about yourself after completing these exercises?
- What action steps will you take based on what you learned this week?

This week has been all about understanding the amazing person you already are. Let this foundation guide your journey toward designing the life you deserve.

II

Week 2-Overcome Self-Doubt: Build Confidence, and Embrace Self-Love

Have you ever looked at someone else and thought, "They're so confident, how do they do it?" Or maybe you've caught yourself wondering, "Am I really good enough to succeed?" You're not alone. Many of us, especially students, face moments when self-doubt creeps in and makes us question our abilities, dreams, and worth.

It could be before a big exam, when preparing for a presentation, or even when deciding what career path to choose. The truth is, self-doubt doesn't just affect adults; it affects students too. Whether you're in high school or college, it's easy to compare yourself to others and feel like you're not measuring up. But here's the thing: self-doubt is normal, and it can be overcome.

In this week, we'll focus on how to shift your mindset, build your confidence, and learn to love yourself for who you truly are. Overcoming self-doubt isn't just about feeling good about yourself in the moment—it's about building a strong foundation of self-belief that will help you take on any challenge with courage and resilience.

Imagine walking into a room, feeling confident in yourself, knowing that you are enough, capable, and deserving of success. That's the power of self-love and confidence. By the end of this week, you will have the tools and mindset to crush your self-doubt and create a more positive, empowered version of yourself.

Objective of the Week

- Recognize and confront your self-doubt.
- Develop strategies to challenge negative thoughts and beliefs.
- Build unshakable confidence and self-love.
- Take actionable steps to improve your mindset and life.

Understanding Self-Doubt and Confidence

Self-doubt is that voice in your head that tells you that you're not good enough, that you can't succeed, or that you're destined to fail. It can be paralyzing, keeping you stuck in inaction and fear. But self-doubt is a normal part of the human experience, and everyone faces it at some point in their lives.

Building confidence is about learning to trust yourself, believe in your abilities, and take action despite fear or uncertainty. Self-love is about accepting yourself, flaws and all, and recognizing that you are worthy of success, happiness, and love.

This week is about understanding where your self-doubt comes from, challenging the negative beliefs that limit you, and replacing them with empowering thoughts and actions.

Activities to Overcome Self-Doubt and Build Confidence

1. Identify Your Self-Doubt Triggers

The first step in overcoming self-doubt is identifying the situations, thoughts, or people that trigger it. Awareness is key to making changes in your mindset.

Instructions

- Sit quietly and reflect on a recent situation where you felt doubt or fear about your abilities.
- Write down the thoughts that went through your mind in that moment (e.g., "I'm not good enough," "I'll never succeed").
- Identify triggers: What caused these thoughts? Was it a specific task, comparison with others, fear of judgment, or a past experience?

Reflection

- What patterns do you notice in your self-doubt?
- Do certain situations, people, or thoughts make it worse?

2. Reframe Negative Thoughts

Once you've identified your self-doubt triggers, the next step is to reframe these negative thoughts into positive, empowering statements. Reframing helps shift your focus from what you can't do to what you can do.

Instructions

- Take the negative thoughts you wrote in the previous activity and turn them into positive affirmations.

For example
Negative Thought: "I'm not capable of succeeding."
Reframed Thought: "I have the skills and resources to succeed, and every effort I make brings me closer to my goal."

Reflection

- How do these reframed thoughts make you feel?
- Can you see how this shift in perspective can impact your actions?

3. Practice Self-Love Daily

Self-love is crucial to building unshakable confidence. It's about acknowledging your worth, **treating yourself with kindness, and**

celebrating your achievements—big and small.
Instructions

- Look at yourself in the mirror each morning and say three things you love about yourself (physical attributes, talents, or qualities).

For example

1. "I love my creativity."
2. "I love my ability to empathize with others."
3. "I love my resilience in tough situations."

- Afterward, take a moment to acknowledge your feelings. Do you feel more connected to yourself?

Reflection

- How does practicing self-love change the way you view yourself?
- Can you identify moments where you have been kind and loving toward yourself in the past?

Interactive Action Plan
Goal Setting for the Week:

1. **Short-Term Goal:** Every day, challenge one negative thought and replace it with a positive affirmation. Keep a journal to track your thoughts and how reframing them makes you feel.
2. **Long-Term Goal:** Over the next few weeks, continue identifying patterns of self-doubt and use your positive affirmations to shift your mindset. Start taking actions to move past your doubts, no matter how small.

Example

When you start doubting your abilities, remind yourself of an achievement, no matter how small it might seem. Then use an affirmation like: "I am capable, and I can handle challenges with grace."

Daily Habit Challenge

- Every morning, say three positive affirmations to yourself and focus on what you love about yourself. Write these in your journal for added reflection.

What You Will Gain?

By the end of Week 2, you will,

1. Understand the root causes of your self-doubt.
2. Have reframed negative thoughts and turned them into empowering affirmations.
3. Build daily self-love practices that help you grow in confidence.
4. Begin to take action, even in the presence of doubt, knowing that you are worthy and capable of achieving your goals.

Closing Thoughts

As we move through this week, remember that overcoming self-doubt is not about being perfect—it's about recognizing your value and moving forward with confidence, no matter the obstacles. Self-love and confidence are practices, and with consistent effort, you can transform your mindset and your life.

Take time each day to affirm your worth, shift your thoughts, and take action on your dreams. With each step, you will continue to build the unshakable confidence you need to face life's challenges and achieve your goals.

Now, grab your pen and book! Start the activities, reflect deeply, and step into the journey of building confidence and embracing self-love today! Week 2 is all about empowering you to trust yourself and your potential. Let's do this!

III

Week 3 – Overcoming Fear: Embracing Courage & Growth

Grab a pen and book right now, and get ready to dive deep into understanding and overcoming your fears. This week, we're going to take action together to break through the fear and emerge stronger and more courageous than ever.

Fear – Something We All Face

Think about the last time you felt scared. Maybe it was before **speaking in front of the class, taking a difficult exam, or trying something new**. Fear is something every one of us experiences. But did you know that fear isn't something you should avoid? Instead, it can be a signal that you're about to do something important—something that will help you grow.

Now, let's be honest: fear can be paralyzing. But here's the secret—the more you face your fears, the more confidence and courage you build. By the end of this week, you'll have the tools and strategies to take charge of your fear and transform it into a force for growth.

What is Fear?

Fear is a natural response to something that feels dangerous, unknown, or threatening. It's the nervousness before a public speech, the anxiousness before an exam, or the hesitation to try something new. But the interesting thing is—fear can also be a sign that you're about to step out of your comfort zone, and that's exactly where growth happens!

Take a moment to reflect

1. What's something you're afraid of?
2. Have you ever felt your heart race, your palms sweat, or your mind go blank in a fearful situation?
3. Did you survive? Yes, you did!

How to Overcome Fear

You don't need to eliminate fear to succeed—you need to learn to move forward in spite of it. Overcoming fear is about building courage and embracing the discomfort that comes with growth.

Here's how you can do it

1. **Acknowledge Your Fear**: Fear becomes more manageable once you recognize it. Admit that you're scared, and don't judge yourself. It's normal. Everyone experiences fear.
2. **Understand Your Fear**: Fear often arises from the unknown or uncertainty. Ask yourself: What's the worst that could happen if I face this fear? Can I handle it?
3. **Reframe Your Fear**: Shift your perspective. Instead of seeing fear as a roadblock, treat it as an opportunity for personal growth. Fear means you're growing, stepping into something new, and becoming stronger.
4. **Take Action**: The best way to overcome fear is to act. Even small steps can make a big difference. Start with one small thing you're afraid to do and take that step today.
5. **Visualize Your Success**: Imagine yourself succeeding. Picture how you'll feel when you overcome the fear. This visual power can help you build

courage and clarity in the moment.

Fear-Busting Tools and Techniques

Here are some tools and techniques that will help you break free from fear and step into your courage.

1. The Courage Journal

Purpose: Helps you understand and release your fear by writing it down.

How to Use: Write about your fears, how they make you feel, and the lessons you're learning. Track your progress as you take action against your fears.

2. The 5-5-7 Breathing Technique

Purpose: Reduces anxiety and calms your mind when fear takes over.
How to Use:

1. Inhale for 5 seconds.
2. Hold your breath for 5 seconds.
3. Exhale for 7 seconds.
4. Repeat this process five times. This helps lower your fear response.

3. Power Poses

Purpose: Increases confidence and courage before facing your fear.

How to Use: Stand like a superhero for 2 minutes (hands on hips, chest open, standing tall). This will trick your brain into thinking you're powerful, reducing fear and boosting your self-belief.

4. Affirmations

Purpose: Rewires your brain to focus on courage and confidence.
How to Use: Write 3 positive affirmations related to facing your fear.

For example, **"I am brave," "I can handle challenges,"** or **"I embrace fear as an opportunity to grow."** Repeat these affirmations aloud each day.

Reflection Questions

Before we move on to activities, take a few moments to reflect on the following questions. Write your answers in your book:

1. What's one fear you're currently facing? (It could be about school, friendships, or stepping out of your comfort zone.)
2. How does this fear make you feel physically? (Do you feel tense, nervous, sweaty, etc.?)
3. What's the worst thing that could happen if you face this fear? (Is it as bad as you imagine?)
4. What's one small step you can take this week to face your fear? (Even the smallest action is a step toward overcoming it.)

Activities: Overcoming Fear

Let's put what we've learned into practice! These activities will help you take actionable steps to face your fear with courage.

Activity 1: Fear-Setting

Instructions:

1. Take a piece of paper and divide it into three columns.
2. In the first column, write down your fear.
3. In the second column, write down the worst-case scenario if you face this fear.
4. In the third column, write down how you can prevent or handle the worst-case scenario.

   Example
   Fear: Speaking in front of the class.
   Worst-case scenario: I forget my lines, and everyone laughs at me.

How to handle it: I'll practice in front of a mirror, focus on key points, and remind myself that everyone makes mistakes.

Activity 2: *Take a Small Step*

Instructions: Identify one small action you can take this week to confront your fear. For example, if you fear speaking in front of the class, your small step might be to volunteer to answer a question in class.

Remember, small steps lead to big results. Write down your action step in your book.

Activity 3: *Affirmation Practice*

Instructions: Write down three affirmations related to overcoming your fear.

For example, **"I am confident," "I am capable of handling any challenge," or "Fear doesn't control me."** Repeat these affirmations aloud every day for the next week.

Action Plan for the Week

1. Write Down Your Fear: Identify one fear you're currently facing.
2. Reframe It: Use the reframing technique to see it as an opportunity for growth.
3. Take Action: Break your fear into small steps and commit to taking one small action this week.
4. Use Your Tools: Apply your Courage Toolkit, including the Courage Journal, breathing technique, power poses, and affirmations.
5. Journal Your Progress: At the end of each day, write about your experiences in your book. How did facing your fear make you feel? What progress did you make?

Summary

Fear is a normal part of life, but it doesn't have to hold you back. By acknowledging it, reframing it, and taking small action steps, you can break through fear and embrace growth. With the tools and techniques we've discussed, you're well on your way to developing unshakable courage. Keep using the tools and continue practicing—you are stronger than you think.

Final Instruction for Students

Now, grab your pen and book once again. Take the first step to overcoming your fear today. Write down your thoughts, fears, and action steps, and start practicing what you've learned. Remember, every step you take will make you braver. Let's start this journey together!

IV

Week 4 – Emotional Intelligence: Understanding and Managing Emotions

Imagine you're preparing for a big exam, and your stress levels are skyrocketing. You can feel your heart racing, your mind going blank, and your emotions are all over the place. How do you respond? Do you panic, or do you take a step back and calm your mind?

Or consider a situation where you're in a group project, and a disagreement occurs. Are you quick to react with frustration, or do you step into the other person's shoes and try to understand their perspective?

Emotional Intelligence (EQ) is about how well you understand and manage your emotions, as well as how you relate to and understand others. As students, it is crucial to know how to handle these emotions in a healthy, constructive way. Managing your stress, building relationships with classmates, and focusing during an exam—all rely on your emotional intelligence.

Take a moment to reflect on these questions

- How do you handle stress during exams or assignments?

- How do you react when your friends or teachers say something that makes you upset?
- When faced with disappointment or failure, do you bounce back quickly or get stuck in negative emotions?

Your ability to manage these emotions will not only help you excel academically but will also shape your relationships and overall happiness.

Why Emotional Intelligence Matters for Students

Emotional Intelligence (EQ) is just as important as traditional intelligence (IQ) when it comes to succeeding in school and in life. EQ can significantly impact how you:

- Manage your emotions during high-pressure situations (like exams or deadlines)
- Navigate social situations and build meaningful relationships
- Handle conflicts with peers or teachers
- Stay motivated and positive in the face of challenges
- Develop self-discipline to stay focused on your goals

The good news? **Emotional Intelligence is a skill you can develop with time and practice.** It doesn't matter if you've struggled with managing your emotions in the past—by learning and practicing the right techniques, you can improve your EQ.

How to Check Your Emotional Intelligence: A Self-Assessment

Start by asking yourself these questions to understand where you stand with your EQ:

1. Self-Awareness

- Can I easily identify what I'm feeling, even in stressful situations?
- Do I recognize how my emotions affect my thoughts, behavior, and decisions?

2. Self-Regulation

- When I'm feeling angry, anxious, or sad, am I able to control my reactions?
- Do I find it easy to stay calm and think clearly during stressful situations like exams or group projects?

3. Empathy

- Do I understand how others are feeling and respond in a supportive way?
- Am I good at listening to my friends, classmates, or teachers when they share their emotions?

4. Social Skills

- Can I communicate my feelings clearly and respectfully?
- Am I able to maintain positive relationships with my peers and teachers?

Tools and Techniques for Improving Your Emotional Intelligence

Now that you know where you stand with your EQ, here are some proven tools and techniques to help you improve each aspect of Emotional Intelligence:

1. Mindfulness and Emotional Awareness

Mindfulness involves paying attention to the present moment without judgment. Being mindful helps you identify and understand your emotions as they arise, allowing you to manage them more effectively.

Activity:

- Take 5 minutes each day to sit in a quiet place. Close your eyes and focus on your breath.
- Notice what emotions come up—do you feel calm, stressed, happy, or anxious?
- Write them down in your notebook. This will help you become more aware of your emotions and triggers.

2. The ABCDE Method for Self-Regulation

The ABCDE method is a great tool for managing negative emotions and transforming your mindset.

1. A: Activating Event (What triggered the emotion?)
2. B: Belief (What did you believe or tell yourself about the event?)
3. C: Consequence (How did this belief make you feel or act?)
4. D: Disputation (Challenge your belief—Was it true or exaggerated?)
5. E: New Effective Belief (Create a healthier belief moving forward)

Example:
If you're stressed about an exam (A), you might think, "I'm going to fail" (B). This could lead to feelings of panic (C). But when you challenge that thought (D) and remind yourself, "I've studied and I'll do my best" (E), you shift your emotions and respond more calmly.

3. Empathy Practice

Empathy is the ability to understand how others feel, even if their emotions differ from your own. By practicing empathy, you improve your relationships and communication skills.

Activity:
The next time a friend or classmate shares something personal, listen without interrupting. Try to understand their emotions by saying things like, "It sounds like you're feeling frustrated because..." This helps you connect on a deeper level.

4. Breathing and Relaxation Techniques

When you're feeling overwhelmed, breathing techniques can help calm your mind and body. Learning how to manage your emotions through breath can boost your emotional control.

Action Plan:

- Practice deep breathing: Inhale for 4 counts, hold for 4, exhale for 4.
- Repeat for 5 minutes, especially before an exam or when feeling stressed.

Action Plan for Improving Your Emotional Intelligence

Here's your action plan for the week to enhance your Emotional Intelligence:

1. Mindfulness and Emotional Awareness

- Spend 5 minutes each day journaling about how you're feeling and why. Reflect on any emotional triggers you may have encountered.

2. Practice Self-Regulation

- Identify situations where you felt your emotions get the best of you. Use the ABCDE method to challenge negative beliefs and develop healthier perspectives.

3. Empathy Practice

- Engage in one conversation per day where you actively listen and empathize with someone's feelings. Make sure to reflect back what you hear to show understanding.

4. Relaxation Techniques

- Incorporate deep breathing or relaxation techniques into your routine to manage stress, especially during exams or challenging situations.

Summary

Improving your Emotional Intelligence will help you better manage stress, understand and control your emotions, and develop stronger relationships with those around you. By applying the tools and techniques shared this week—such as mindfulness, the ABCDE method, and empathy practice—you'll build a foundation for handling life's challenges in a healthier, more constructive way.

Reflection and Takeaways

Before we wrap up, take a moment to reflect:

1. What emotions did you notice this week?
2. How did you respond to those emotions?
3. Which tool or technique are you most excited to apply next?
4. What is one actionable step you'll take this week to improve your Emotional Intelligence?

Remember, developing Emotional Intelligence is a process, and by practicing these steps consistently, you will see growth in how you manage yourself and interact with others. Keep tracking your progress and be patient with yourself.

V

Week 5 – Healthy Relationships: Setting Boundaries and Practicing Self-Respect

Why Healthy Relationships Matter

Imagine this: You're helping a friend with their homework even though you have an important assignment due tomorrow. You agreed because you didn't want to upset them, but now you feel stressed and resentful. Have you ever been in a situation like this?

Or maybe you have a friend who constantly asks for favors but rarely offers help in return. You feel **uncomfortable saying "no,"** but deep down, you know the relationship feels one-sided.

Healthy relationships are built on mutual respect, understanding, and boundaries. Whether it's with friends, family, teachers, or even yourself, knowing how to set boundaries and practice self-respect is key to maintaining balance and happiness in your life.

Take a moment to reflect

1. Do you often feel drained or stressed because of your relationships?
2. Do you struggle to say "no" to others, even when you want to?
3. Do you feel respected and valued in your friendships and relationships?

By learning how to set boundaries and respect yourself, you can build healthier, happier relationships.

What Are Healthy Relationships?

A healthy relationship is one where:

1. **Mutual Respect**: Both people value and respect each other's feelings, needs, and opinions.
2. **Trust and Honesty**: There's open communication without fear of judgment or dishonesty.
3. **Boundaries**: Each person has their personal space, time, and emotional limits respected.
4. **Support**: You feel uplifted, encouraged, and safe in the relationship.

In contrast, unhealthy relationships often involve

- Feeling controlled, disrespected, or undervalued.
- Fear of expressing your true thoughts and emotions.
- Constant stress or negativity from the other person.

Why Are Boundaries and Self-Respect Important?

1. **Prevents Burnout:** Constantly giving without setting limits can leave you emotionally and physically drained.
2. **Boosts Self-Esteem**: Standing up for your needs reinforces your self-worth.
3. **Encourages Respect from Others:** When you respect yourself, others are more likely to respect you.

4. **Creates Balance:** Boundaries ensure that relationships are healthy and mutually beneficial.

How to Check the Health of Your Relationships

Ask yourself these questions:

- Do I feel respected and valued by this person?
- Can I express my feelings and opinions without fear?
- Does this person support me during difficult times?
- Do I feel comfortable saying "no" to this person?

If the answers are mostly "no," it's a sign that the relationship may need healthier boundaries or reevaluation.

Tools and Techniques for Setting Boundaries and Practicing Self-Respect

1. Understand Your Limits

- Reflect on what makes you feel uncomfortable or stressed in relationships. Write down situations where you felt your boundaries were crossed.

2. Learn to Say "No"

- Practice saying "no" in a polite but firm way.
- Example: "I'd love to help, but I have my own deadlines to meet."

3. Communicate Clearly

- Use "I" statements to express your feelings and needs without blaming the other person.
- Example: "I feel overwhelmed when I'm expected to take on extra tasks. I need to focus on my priorities."

4. Practice Self-Respect

- Treat yourself kindly, just as you would a friend.
- Celebrate your achievements, big or small.
- Don't compromise your values to please others.

5. Detach from Toxic Relationships

- If a relationship consistently makes you feel bad about yourself, it might be time to distance yourself or let go.

Activities for Building Healthy Relationships

1. Boundary Mapping

- Take a pen and notebook.
- Write down situations where you feel your boundaries are often crossed.
- Reflect on how you can respond differently in these situations to protect your boundaries.

2. The "Respect Checklist"

- List all the important relationships in your life.
- For each one, check: Do I feel respected? Am I able to set boundaries?

- Identify one relationship where you want to work on boundaries and write down an action plan.

3. Role-Playing

- Pair up with a friend or practice alone.
- Practice saying "no" or setting a boundary in a scenario you find challenging.
- Example: "I understand you need help, but I'm not available right now. Let's find another time."

4. Gratitude for Healthy Relationships

- Write a letter to someone who supports and respects you. Reflect on how their presence adds value to your life.

Action Plan for the Week

1. Identify Unhealthy Patterns:

- Reflect on your relationships and identify situations where you need to set boundaries.

2. Practice Setting Boundaries:

- Choose one situation this week where you will practice saying "no" or communicating your needs.

3. Focus on Self-Respect:

- Spend time doing activities that boost your self-esteem—write affirmations, journal about your strengths, or treat yourself kindly.

4. Strengthen Healthy Relationships:

- Reach out to someone who respects and supports you. Spend quality time with them and express your gratitude.

Summary: Key Takeaways

Healthy relationships are built on mutual respect, trust, and boundaries. By setting clear limits and practicing self-respect, you can protect your emotional well-being and foster balanced, positive connections with others.

Remember

1. It's okay to say "no" when you need to.
2. Communicating your needs doesn't make you selfish—it makes you strong.
3. Self-respect is the foundation of every healthy relationship.

Reflection and Final Thoughts

Take a moment to reflect:

1. Which relationship in your life needs healthier boundaries?
2. What is one step you'll take this week to set boundaries?
3. How will practicing self-respect improve your relationships and overall well-being?

With practice, you'll find that healthy relationships are not only possible but also deeply rewarding. Keep working on these tools, and you'll notice a positive change in how you connect with others—and with yourself.

VI
Week 6- Health and Wellness: Balancing Mind, Body, and Spirit

Refresh, Reset, Restart Your Life

As a student, you're constantly on the go—studying, attending classes, meeting deadlines, and juggling social activities. It can be easy to feel drained, disconnected, or overwhelmed by everything on your plate. But what if you could refresh, reset, and restart your life by finding balance in the three most important aspects of your well-being: your mind, body, and spirit?

Balancing these three areas is not just about avoiding burnout—it's about setting yourself up for long-term success and happiness. When you take time to care for your mind, body, and spirit, you'll feel more energized, focused, and equipped to face life's challenges. Imagine starting each day feeling grounded, centered, and ready to take on anything.

This week, we'll explore how to achieve that balance, and why it's so essential for students like you. You'll learn simple, actionable strategies to take care of yourself in a way that improves your mental clarity, physical health, and emotional resilience.

Why Balance is Important for Students?

As a student, you face unique challenges: the pressure of exams, the stress of assignments, and the need to juggle school with your social life and personal growth. It's easy to become overwhelmed. But when your mind, body, and spirit are aligned, you'll find that you not only cope better with stress but also perform better academically and socially.

Here's how balancing these aspects can help you

- **Mental Clarity:** A balanced mind helps you stay focused and sharp, making studying easier and more effective.
- **Physical Health**: When you take care of your body, you have more energy and resilience, which is essential for tackling long study sessions or physical activities.
- **Emotional Strength:** Taking care of your spirit helps you stay calm, confident, and emotionally steady, no matter the circumstances.

By focusing on all three, you'll cultivate overall wellness and avoid burnout—something every student can benefit from!

How to Incorporate Balance into Your Daily Routine?

Balancing mind, body, and spirit doesn't have to be complicated. The key is to make small, intentional choices each day that nurture all three areas. Here's how you can start:

1. Mind: Practice Mindfulness

Mindfulness is about being present in the moment. It helps calm your mind, reduces stress, and boosts focus. You don't have to meditate for hours—just a few minutes each day can make a huge difference.

How to practice:

- Start your day with 5 minutes of mindful breathing or a short meditation. Focus on your breath, and whenever your mind wanders, gently bring it back.

- During study breaks, take a moment to stretch and check in with how you're feeling—both mentally and emotionally.

2. Body: Stay Active and Nourished

Your body needs movement and proper nourishment to stay strong and energized. Physical activity doesn't have to be a long workout session; it can be as simple as a walk or stretching. Also, fueling your body with healthy food makes a world of difference in how you feel physically and mentally.
How to stay active:

- Set aside 15-20 minutes a day for physical activity. Try a quick workout, stretching, or even dancing to your favorite music!
- Drink plenty of water and eat nutritious meals to keep your body energized throughout the day.

3. Spirit: Cultivate Inner Peace and Purpose

Balancing your spirit is about nurturing your emotional and spiritual well-being. It's about understanding your values, practicing gratitude, and connecting to your sense of purpose.
How to nurture your spirit:

- Begin each day with gratitude. Write down 3 things you're thankful for, even if they're small.
- Reflect on your passions, values, and what truly matters to you. Doing this helps you stay grounded and connected to your sense of purpose.

Activities for Mind, Body, and Spirit

Mind Activities

- **Mindful Journaling**: Write for 5 minutes about how you're feeling today. What's on your mind? What are you looking forward to? This practice helps you process thoughts and reduce mental clutter.
- **Visualization**: Take 3 minutes to close your eyes and visualize a peaceful scene—a beach, a forest, or any place that brings you calm. Imagine yourself being fully immersed in that environment.

Body Activities

- **Stretching**: Dedicate 5-10 minutes a day to stretching. Stretching releases tension and improves flexibility.
- **Movement Breaks**: During your study sessions, set a timer to remind you to get up and move every 30-60 minutes. This helps with circulation and mental clarity.

Spirit Activities

- **Gratitude Practice**: Each morning or night, write down 3 things you are grateful for. This simple practice shifts your focus from what's going wrong to what's going right.
- **Meditation or Mindfulness**: Spend 5-10 minutes a day sitting quietly, focusing on your breath. This helps you stay calm and centered.
- **Acts of Kindness**: Spread positivity! Do something kind for someone every day, whether it's a compliment, helping a friend, or simply listening. Acts of kindness build emotional strength and increase feelings of connectedness.

Action Plan

1. Choose One Focus for Each Area

- Choose one practice for each area—mind, body, and spirit—that resonates with you. Whether it's meditation for your mind, stretching for your body, or gratitude for your spirit, start with one area and build from there.

2. Set a Daily Routine

- Dedicate 15-30 minutes each day to these practices. Consistency is key! Try starting your day with a mindfulness practice, then incorporate physical activity and spiritual reflection throughout the day.

3. Track Your Progress

- Keep a journal to reflect on your progress. Note how you feel physically, mentally, and emotionally after each activity. This will help you see the improvements and stay motivated.

Summary

Balancing your mind, body, and spirit is a powerful way to feel more aligned, focused, and energized. When you nurture each of these areas, you set yourself up for success—not just in your studies, but in your overall well-being.

Remember, you don't have to be perfect. Start small, stay consistent, and gradually build up your daily practices. As you incorporate these activities into your routine, you'll notice how much more centered, peaceful, and productive you become.

So take a moment today to reset your mind, body, and spirit. You have the tools to live a balanced, healthy life, and this week is your opportunity to begin.

VII

Week7-Design Your Dream Career and Achieve Financial Independence

Imagine waking up every day excited about what you do, knowing that you're building a career that not only makes you happy but also leads you to financial freedom. Does that sound too good to be true? Well, it's possible! This week, we're going to explore how you can design your dream career, achieve financial independence, and build a life you love.

We will talk about Ikigai, Multiple Intelligences, and Robert Kiyosaki's Cash Flow Quadrant. These tools will help you identify your purpose, match your career to your natural talents, and set a path to financial freedom. Most importantly, we'll discuss how your career can be enjoyable and aligned with your passions, skills, and financial goals.

Let's dive into how you can start shaping your dream career!

Understanding Ikigai – Your Reason for Being

Ikigai is a Japanese concept that refers to the intersection of four key elements in life:

1. What you love (your passions)

2. What you are good at (your talents)

3. What the world needs (your purpose)

4. What you can be paid for (your profession)

Why Ikigai Matters for Your Career

- By finding your Ikigai, you can align your work with what excites you.
- It helps you to discover a career that blends passion, talent, and purpose with financial sustainability.
- It ensures you're not just working for money, but working for fulfillment and making a difference.

Activity

Take a moment to reflect on the four elements of Ikigai and write down your answers for each one:

1. What do you love doing?
2. What are you good at?
3. What does the world need more of?
4. What can you get paid for?

After answering, find the intersection between these answers. That's your Ikigai!

Exploring Multiple Intelligences for Career Fit

Howard Gardner's theory of Multiple Intelligences suggests that there are different ways people excel. Everyone has unique strengths, and identifying your dominant type of intelligence can help you choose a career path that is more enjoyable and fulfilling.

Here are the 9 types of Multiple Intelligences and career options that suit each

1. Linguistic Intelligence (Word Smart)

Description: Ability to express oneself through words.
Career Options: Writer, journalist, lawyer, teacher, public speaker.

2. Logical-Mathematical Intelligence (Logic Smart)

Description: Ability to think logically and solve mathematical problems.
Career Options: Scientist, engineer, computer programmer, financial analyst.

3. Spatial Intelligence (Picture Smart)

Description: Ability to think in images and pictures.
Career Options: Architect, graphic designer, photographer, artist.

4. Bodily-Kinesthetic Intelligence (Body Smart)

Description: Ability to control body movements and handle objects skillfully.
Career Options: Athlete, surgeon, dancer, physical therapist.

5. Musical Intelligence (Music Smart)

Description: Ability to understand and create music.
Career Options: Musician, composer, sound engineer, music teacher.

6. Interpersonal Intelligence (People Smart)

Description: Ability to understand and interact effectively with others.
Career Options: Psychologist, counselor, teacher, manager, sales representative.

7. Intrapersonal Intelligence (Self Smart)

Description: Ability to understand oneself and one's emotions.
Career Options: Life coach, philosopher, writer, counselor.

8. Naturalistic Intelligence (Nature Smart)

Description: Ability to recognize and categorize natural elements.

Career Options: Environmentalist, biologist, farmer, wildlife photographer.

9. Existential Intelligence (Big Picture Smart)

- Description: Ability to ponder deep questions about life, death, and existence.
- Career Options: Philosopher, theologian, counselor, spiritual leader.

Activity

Reflect on your dominant intelligence and choose a career option that fits. Write down how you can develop and use your strengths to choose a meaningful career.

Robert Kiyosaki's Cash Flow Quadrant: Understanding Career Choices and Financial Freedom

Robert Kiyosaki's Cash Flow Quadrant helps you understand the different ways people earn money and how they impact your financial freedom. The quadrant is divided into four categories: Employee (E), Self-Employed (S), Business Owner (B), and Investor (I).

1. Employee (E): You work for a salary and are dependent on your employer for income.

Career Example: Office worker, teacher, doctor.

2. Self-Employed (S): You work for yourself and control your income.

Career Example: Freelancer, consultant, small business owner.

3. Business Owner (B): You create a business that works for you and generates passive income.

Career Example: Owner of a large business or franchise.

4. Investor (I): Your money works for you, and you earn through investments.

Career Example: Real estate investor, stock market investor.

Why This Matters

Your goal should be to move from the E and S quadrants (where your time is directly linked to your income) into the B and I quadrants (where your wealth grows without directly tying your time to income).

This transition can lead you to financial freedom by learning how to leverage your skills and invest wisely.

Activity:

- Analyze where you are in the Cash Flow Quadrant today.
- Reflect on where you want to be in the future.
- Start thinking about how you can make a move toward the B or I quadrants by building systems or investing money.

Managing Your Money for Financial Freedom

To achieve financial freedom, it's crucial to understand how to manage your money well. This involves:

- **Budgeting**: Track your income and expenses to avoid unnecessary spending.
- **Saving**: Set aside a portion of your income for emergencies and future investments.
- **Investing**: Start investing in stocks, real estate, or other income-generating assets.
- **Understanding Taxes and Debt**: Learn how to manage debt and minimize tax liabilities to keep more of your earnings.

Activity:

- Create a simple budget plan for yourself.
- Write down your monthly income and categorize your expenses (**needs, wants, savings, etc.**).
- Identify areas where you can save and invest for the future.

Summary

This week, we explored how to design your dream career by aligning it with your Ikigai and Multiple Intelligences, and how to understand the financial implications of different career paths using Robert Kiyosaki's Cash Flow Quadrant. We also learned how to manage money effectively to build financial independence.

Remember, your career should not only align with your talents and passions but also lead you toward financial freedom. As you explore career options, consider using your strengths and looking for ways to leverage your skills, build systems, and invest wisely.

Action Plan

1. **Identify your Ikigai** — what you love, what you're good at, what the world needs, and what you can be paid for.
2. **Reflect on your Multiple Intelligence** and choose career options that suit your natural strengths.
3. **Understand where you are in the Cash Flow Quadrant** and start planning how to move toward the B and I quadrants for financial freedom.
4. Take charge of your **money management** by budgeting, saving, and investing.
5. **Regularly review your career path and financial progress** to ensure you're staying on track for success.

Now, take your pen and notebook and start reflecting on your career choices, skills, and financial goals. Write down your thoughts, dreams, and action steps as you design the career and life you truly want!

VIII

Week 8-The Power of Goal Setting:Dream, Plan, Achieve

Have you ever wondered how some people achieve their dreams while others struggle to make progress? The key to success lies in goal setting! Setting clear, actionable goals is like having a roadmap that leads you from where you are to where you want to be. In this week, we'll explore the power of goal setting, how it can transform your dreams into reality, and how to break down your goals into achievable steps.

Goal setting helps you stay focused, motivated, and on track. When you create a dream plan and work towards it, you are essentially creating the life you envision. It's time to turn your dreams into clear, actionable goals and create a path that leads to success. Let's discover how you can achieve anything you set your mind to!

The Importance of Goal Setting

Goal setting is one of the most powerful tools to direct your energy and actions toward achieving your desired outcomes. Without clear goals, it's easy to feel lost or unsure of what to focus on. Setting goals provides you with direction, a sense of purpose, and motivation.

Here's why goal setting is important

1. **Gives you clarity**: Clear goals help you know exactly what you want to achieve.
2. **Motivates you**: Working towards a goal can be exciting and help you stay motivated.
3. **Measurable progress**: Goals allow you to track progress and celebrate small wins along the way.
4. **Boosts confidence**: Achieving goals boosts your self-esteem and shows you that you can accomplish what you set out to do.

The Process of Goal Setting

Step 1: Dream Big – Think About What You Really Want

- Start by thinking about your long-term dreams. This could include academic goals, career goals, personal growth, relationships, health, or financial aspirations. Dream big, without limiting yourself!

Step 2: Make It SMART

To make your dreams achievable, break them down into SMART goals. SMART stands for:

- **S**pecific: Be clear and precise about what you want.
- **M**easurable: Define how you will measure progress or success.
- **A**chievable: Make sure the goal is realistic and possible to achieve.
- **R**elevant: Ensure that the goal is meaningful and aligned with your bigger purpose.
- **T**ime-Bound: Set a timeline for when you want to achieve the goal.

Example of a SMART Goal

- **Goal:** I want to improve my grades in math.
- **SMART Goal**: I will study math for 1 hour every day for 30 days and aim to raise my grade from C to B+ by the end of the month.

Step 3: Break It Down into Actionable Steps

- Once you have a SMART goal, break it down into smaller, manageable tasks. This makes the goal feel less overwhelming and gives you a clear plan of action.

For example, if your goal is to improve your grades, your tasks might include:

1. Attend all math classes.
2. Dedicate 1 hour per day to reviewing notes.
3. Solve practice problems daily.
4. Ask for help when struggling with a topic.

Step 4: Take Action and Stay Consistent

- The most important part of achieving your goals is taking consistent action. Set aside time each day or week to work on your goals. Remember, every small step adds up!

Step 5: Monitor Your Progress and Adjust as Needed

- Regularly check your progress to see if you're moving closer to your goal. If something isn't working, adjust your approach and try new strategies.

Types of Goals Students Should Focus On

1. **Academic Goals**: Improve grades, complete assignments on time, study more efficiently.
2. **Personal Growth Goals**: Build confidence, improve communication skills, develop emotional intelligence.
3. **Health & Wellness Goals**: Eat healthier, exercise regularly, maintain a balanced lifestyle.
4. **Career Goals**: Explore career options, gain new skills, take internships or work experience.
5. **Financial Goals**: Save money, budget effectively, plan for future financial independence.

Visualizing Your Success: The Power of a Vision Board

A vision board is a powerful tool for visualizing your goals. It's a collage of images, words, and affirmations that represent your dreams and the future you want to create. By looking at your vision board every day, you are reinforcing your goals and staying focused on what you want to achieve.

How to Create Your Vision Board

1. Collect magazines, print images, or use online resources to find pictures that represent your dreams and goals.
2. Cut them out and glue them onto a board or poster.
3. Arrange the images in a way that feels inspiring and motivating.
4. Add words, quotes, and affirmations that encourage you.
5. Display your vision board somewhere you can see it every day.

Looking at this vision board will serve as a reminder of where you're headed and why you are working toward your goals.

The Power of Affirmations

Affirmations are positive statements that can reprogram your mind to believe in your potential and capabilities. Repeating affirmations helps you overcome negative thoughts, stay focused on your goals, and boost your confidence.

Examples of Goal-Oriented Affirmations

1. "I am capable of achieving my goals and dreams."
2. "Every day, I am getting closer to my ideal career."
3. "I am confident in my abilities to succeed."
4. "I attract success and abundance into my life."

To use affirmations effectively

- Write them down.
- Say them aloud every day.
- Visualize yourself achieving the goal while repeating the affirmation.

Activity 1: Creating Your Dream List

Take a moment to reflect on what you want to achieve in the next 1 year, 5 years, and 10 years. Write down your dreams and aspirations in these categories:

- Personal goals (e.g., self-love, confidence)
- Academic goals (e.g., grades, subjects to master)
- Career goals (e.g., what kind of work do you want to do?)
- Health goals (e.g., fitness, diet)
- Financial goals (e.g., savings, investments)

Activity 2: Setting SMART Goals

- Now that you have your dream list, choose one goal and convert it into a SMART goal. Use the framework and create a clear, actionable plan for how you can achieve it.

Activity 3: Create Your Vision Board

Create your vision board, either physically with magazines or digitally using online tools like Canva. Be creative and include images, words, and quotes that resonate with your dreams.

Reflection:

- Take some time to reflect on the following:
- Why do you think setting goals is important for your success?
- How do you feel when you achieve a goal?
- What is one goal you would like to work on this week? What steps can you take today to move toward it?

Overcoming Obstacles and Staying Motivated

Achieving goals isn't always easy. Sometimes, obstacles may come your way, and motivation may dip. Here are some tips to stay on track:

1. Celebrate Small Wins: Recognize and celebrate your progress, no matter how small.

2. Stay Positive: Keep a positive attitude even when things get tough.

3. Find Support: Talk to someone about your goals — friends, family, or a mentor.

4. Visualize Your Success: Imagine the feeling of achieving your goal and use that as motivation.

5. Learn from Mistakes: If you face setbacks, don't give up. Learn from them and keep moving forward.

Final Thoughts

This week, you learned that setting clear, specific goals is the foundation of success. By dreaming big, planning smart, and taking action, you can make your goals a reality. Remember, it's not just about dreaming — it's about putting in the effort, tracking your progress, and staying consistent. With the power of goal setting, you can achieve anything you set your mind to!

Action Plan

1. Create your dream list.
2. Choose one goal and break it down into a SMART goal.
3. Create your vision board.
4. Start working on the actionable steps to achieve your goal.
5. Track your progress and adjust when necessary.
6. Reflect on your progress weekly and celebrate your small wins.

Now, go ahead and start designing your future with clear, actionable goals. Remember, your dreams are within reach — **all you need is a solid plan, daily visualization, and consistent action to make them come true!**

IX

Week9-Master Your Time: Boost Productivity and Beat Procrastination

Do you ever feel like there aren't enough hours in the day? Between school, homework, extracurricular activities, and personal time, it often feels like time slips away before we can even begin to accomplish everything we want. But the good news is: you can take control of your time! Time management is a superpower that can help you achieve your goals, reduce stress, and lead a balanced life.

In this chapter, we will explore time management techniques that will help you stop procrastinating, boost your productivity, and make the most of every minute. Whether you're in school, college, or even balancing work and study, these tools will help you manage your time like a pro.

Understanding Time Management

Time management is all about prioritizing your tasks, organizing your day, and using your time in the best way possible. Good time management means you'll spend less time stressing and more time achieving.

Why is time management so important?

1. **Reduced Stress:** When you know exactly what to do and when to do it, there's no last-minute rush.
2. **Increased Productivity**: You'll complete tasks quicker and more efficiently.
3. **More Free Time:** Good time management allows you to enjoy your personal time and pursue hobbies or relaxation.
4. Effective time management can help you turn your dreams into reality, one task at a time!

What is Procrastination and Why Do We Do It?

Procrastination happens when we delay tasks, especially the ones we don't enjoy, until the last minute. Sometimes, procrastination is caused by fear of failure, perfectionism, or feeling overwhelmed. Here's the reality: everyone procrastinates at some point. But the trick is knowing how to break free from it.

Reasons we procrastinate

1. **Fear of failure**: You may avoid starting something because you're worried you won't do it perfectly.
2. **Lack of motivation:** When a task doesn't excite you, it's easy to put it off.
3. **Overwhelm:** When a task feels too big or too hard, procrastination seems like a way to escape the pressure.
4. **Distractions**: Social media, video games, or even just chatting with friends can pull you away from your goals.

How to Overcome Procrastination

Procrastination can be defeated. All it takes is changing your approach and using a few strategies to stay focused.

1. Break Down Big Tasks

A huge project can seem intimidating, but breaking it down into smaller, manageable steps makes it feel less overwhelming. For example, instead of writing an entire essay in one go, divide it into stages: research, outline, writing, and editing.

2. Set Short-Term Goals

Create small, specific goals for each task. These goals can give you a clear direction and make your tasks feel more achievable.

3. Use the "5-Minute Rule"

Commit to working on a task for just five minutes. Once you start, you'll often find it easier to keep going. You'll build momentum and get more done than you thought!

4. Remove Distractions

Turn off your phone, close social media, or find a quiet space. By eliminating distractions, you can focus better and finish your tasks faster.

5. Celebrate Small Wins

Reward yourself when you complete a task or achieve a goal. This will motivate you to keep going and help break the cycle of procrastination.

Mastering Time Management

Now that you've learned how to beat procrastination, let's dive into how to manage your time effectively:

1. Prioritize Your Tasks

Use the Eisenhower Matrix to prioritize what's most important:

1. **Urgent & Important:** Do these tasks immediately.
2. **Important but Not Urgent:** Schedule these tasks for later.
3. **Urgent but Not Important:** Delegate or ask for help with these tasks.

4. **Neither Urgent nor Important:** Eliminate or ignore these tasks.

By focusing on what truly matters, you'll avoid wasting time on tasks that don't move you closer to your goals.

2. Time Blocking

Time blocking is a simple yet powerful technique where you schedule specific blocks of time for each task or activity. For example, dedicate one hour for studying, then take a 20-minute break before moving to your next task. This keeps you focused and organized throughout the day.

3. Use a Planner or Digital Tools

Whether you prefer a physical planner or an app, keeping track of your schedule is key. Write down your to-dos, deadlines, and goals for the day or week. This will help you visualize your tasks and stay on top of them.

4. Create a Routine

Having a consistent routine will help you stay organized and efficient. Set aside time for studying, hobbies, meals, and relaxation. A structured day helps you stay on track and reduces stress.

Boosting Your Productivity

Being productive is about working smarter, not harder. Here are some tips to help you get more done in less time:

1. The Pomodoro Technique

This technique involves working for 25 minutes and then taking a 5-minute break. After four sessions, take a longer break (15-30 minutes). It helps you stay focused and prevents burnout.

2. Batch Similar Tasks Together

Grouping similar tasks together can save you time and energy. For instance, if you have to make a lot of calls, do them all in one go instead of spreading them throughout the day.

3. Avoid Multitasking

Multitasking can lower your efficiency. Focus on one task at a time, and you'll find you get more done in less time.

4. Use Tools to Enhance Focus

Apps like Forest, Focus@Will, or StayFocusd can block distractions and keep you focused on your tasks. These tools help you avoid wasting time on social media or other non-essential activities.

The Power of Time Reflection

Take a moment each week to reflect on how you've spent your time. Did you accomplish what you set out to do? Were there any time-wasters? This reflection will help you identify what's working and what's not, so you can adjust your strategy.

Building a Productive Mindset:

A productive mindset is the belief that you can use your time wisely and achieve your goals. Here's how to build one:

1. Start with Small Wins

Set small goals that you know you can achieve. Completing these goals will build your confidence and motivate you to take on bigger tasks.

2. Embrace Challenges

Don't shy away from difficult tasks. A productive mindset involves seeing challenges as opportunities for growth.

3. Visualize Your Success

Imagine yourself achieving your goals. Visualizing success helps you stay focused and reminds you of why you're putting in the effort.

Key Takeaways

- Procrastination is normal, but it can be managed with the right strategies, such as breaking tasks into smaller steps and using the Pomodoro Technique.
- Effective time management involves prioritizing tasks, creating a routine, and using tools to stay organized.
- Boost your productivity by batching tasks, avoiding multitasking, and focusing on one task at a time.
- Reflect on how you spend your time each week to ensure you're using it effectively.
- A productive mindset helps you stay motivated, overcome challenges, and achieve your goals.

Conclusion

Time is your most valuable resource. By managing it wisely, you can achieve your goals, reduce stress, and create a balanced life. Mastering time management doesn't happen overnight, but with consistent effort and the right strategies, you'll be able to take control of your time and get more done. Remember, it's not about having more time; it's about using the time you have in the best way possible.

Keep moving forward, and remember—time is on your side when you manage it well!

X

Week 10-Overcome Challenges: Building Mental Toughness and Resilience

Life is full of challenges, and everyone, from school students to young adults in college, faces them at some point. Whether it's a tough subject, peer pressure, personal struggles, or self-doubt, the ability to overcome challenges determines our future success. But here's the good news: mental toughness and resilience are skills that can be developed with practice!

In this week, we will explore how to build these powerful qualities, making you stronger, more adaptable, and ready to face whatever life throws at you. You'll learn actionable steps, fun exercises, and get to create your own personalized action plan to build the mental strength you need.

What is Mental Toughness and Resilience?

Mental Toughness: This is your ability to stay focused, stay positive, and keep going, even when things get tough. It's like the "inner strength" that helps you push through difficulties without giving up.

Resilience: Resilience is your ability to bounce back after facing setbacks or challenges. It's about being able to recover and keep moving forward, no matter how many times you fall.

Why Are Mental Toughness and Resilience Important?

- **Confidence Booster**: The stronger your mindset, the more confident you'll feel when taking on challenges.
- **Stress Management**: A resilient person doesn't crumble under pressure but stays calm and collected.
- **Long-Term Success**: You'll find it easier to achieve your goals if you're not afraid to fail and can bounce back after setbacks.
- **Personal Growth**: Every challenge you face is an opportunity to grow stronger and wiser.

The Power of a Positive Mindset

To develop mental toughness and resilience, it's essential to adopt a positive mindset. This mindset helps you focus on the opportunities, not the obstacles, and see challenges as opportunities to grow.

Growth Mindset vs Fixed Mindset

- **Growth Mindset**: This mindset embraces challenges as chances to improve. People with this mindset believe they can always grow through effort and learning.
- **Fixed Mindset**: People with a fixed mindset think abilities and intelligence are static. They may shy away from challenges and give up easily when things get tough.

Action Steps to Build Mental Toughness and Resilience

1. Develop Self-Discipline

Discipline is the foundation of mental toughness. Whether it's doing your homework on time, practicing a new skill, or following through on your commitments, self-discipline will help you build resilience.

Activity: Goal Setting for Self-Discipline

- **What to Do**: Write down three goals you want to accomplish this week, such as finishing homework by a certain time, practicing a new skill, or sticking to a routine.
- **Action Plan**: Break these goals into daily tasks. Keep track of your progress by checking them off each day.
- **Engagement Tip**: Reward yourself with a fun activity once you complete your goals!

2. Learn to Manage Your Emotions

Being mentally tough doesn't mean suppressing emotions. It means learning to manage them so they don't control you when stress or adversity hits.

Activity: Emotion Check-In

- **What to Do**: Every morning, take 2 minutes to check in with your emotions. Write down how you're feeling and why.
- **Action Plan:** When you face a tough situation, pause and notice your emotions. Take deep breaths and choose a positive response instead of reacting impulsively.
- **Engagement Tip**: Share your emotional check-ins with a friend or family member. It helps to talk it out!

3. Focus on What You Can Control

When facing difficulties, focus on what you can control: your effort, attitude, and actions. Don't waste energy on things beyond your control.

Activity: Control Circle

- **What to Do**: Draw a circle on paper. Inside the circle, write things you can control (e.g., your effort, attitude). Outside the circle, write things you can't control (e.g., other people's opinions, unexpected events).

- **Action Plan**: Commit to focusing only on what's inside the circle. Each time you start worrying about things outside the circle, bring your focus back to what you can control.
- **Engagement Tip**: Share your circle with a friend or parent and ask them what they would write inside their control circle!

4. Embrace Failure as a Learning Opportunity

Failure is a part of life. What matters is how you respond to it. Mentally tough individuals see failure as an opportunity to learn, grow, and come back stronger.

Activity: Reflecting on Failures

- **What to Do**: Think of a time you failed or didn't succeed as planned. Write about the experience and what you learned from it.
- **Action Plan**: Next time you face a challenge, remind yourself that failure is not the end. It's just a lesson in disguise.
- **Engagement Tip**: Share your learning experience with someone you trust. It will help you gain a fresh perspective.

Building Resilience

Resilience is your ability to bounce back and keep moving forward, no matter how many times you fall. Here are ways to strengthen your resilience:

1. Develop Emotional Awareness

Being aware of your emotions helps you process them in a healthy way. Resilient people know how to handle tough emotions without letting them control their actions.

Activity: Emotional Awareness Journal

- **What to Do**: At the end of each day, reflect on your emotions and what caused them. Were you happy, angry, sad, or stressed? Write about it.

- **Action Plan**: Use your journal to identify patterns and triggers. Each time you feel overwhelmed, refer to your journal to understand and manage your emotions better.

2. Strengthen Your Support System

Building resilience doesn't mean doing it all alone. Surround yourself with positive, supportive people who will encourage you and help you bounce back from tough times.

Activity: Identify Your Support Team

- **What to Do**: Write down the names of friends, family members, or mentors you can rely on during tough times.
- **Action Plan**: The next time you feel down or face a challenge, reach out to someone from your support team.

3. Stay Flexible and Adaptable

Life is unpredictable, and resilience requires the ability to adapt when plans don't go as expected. Don't get stuck in one way of thinking—be open to change and new solutions.

Activity: Adaptability Challenge

- **What to Do**: Try something new each week that challenges your usual routine or comfort zone. It could be a new study method, a new hobby, or even a change in your schedule.
- **Action Plan**: Be mindful of your ability to adapt. Celebrate your flexibility and how it helps you grow.

Building Mental Toughness and Resilience – Your Action Plan

- **Create a Daily Practice**: Start each day with a positive affirmation or goal setting. This could be a simple mantra like, "I am strong, and I can overcome any challenge."

- **Develop Habits for Mental Toughness:** Incorporate activities like mindfulness, deep breathing, or journaling to keep your mind resilient and focused.
- **Seek Support:** Surround yourself with people who encourage you, and don't hesitate to reach out when you need help.
- **Celebrate Small Wins:** Each time you overcome a challenge, even a small one, celebrate it. This will boost your confidence and keep you motivated to keep going.

Key Takeaways

- Mental toughness and resilience are essential skills for overcoming challenges and growing stronger.
- To build these skills, focus on self-discipline, emotional management, and growth mindset.
- Embrace challenges as opportunities, learn from failures, and keep moving forward.
- Surround yourself with supportive people and stay adaptable to life's changes.

Conclusion

You've just learned that overcoming challenges is all about how you respond to them. Mental toughness and resilience are not something you're born with—they can be built and developed over time with practice and patience. Keep embracing challenges, stay focused on what you can control, and never give up on yourself. Your ability to handle tough situations will determine how high you soar in life. Keep going—you've got this!

XI

Week11-Create Your Perfect Daily Routine: The Power of Self-Discipline and Building Habits

Welcome to this transformative week where we'll design a daily routine that sets you up for success, fuels your growth, and helps you stay focused on your goals. By incorporating what we've already learned in previous weeks about mindset, self-love, goal-setting, and healthy living, we'll create a routine that not only helps you manage time but also empowers you to become the best version of yourself.

You have the power to design your life—your routine is the blueprint. Your daily habits will shape your success, mindset, and ultimately, your future. Whether you're a student juggling schoolwork, extracurricular activities, or planning for your future, this chapter will guide you to build a daily routine that works for YOU.

Ready to take control of your day? Let's get started! Grab your pen, a notebook, and let's create your perfect daily routine that will help you achieve your dreams and goals.

The Power of Self-Discipline and Habits

Self-discipline is the ability to stay focused and push yourself to take action regardless of emotional state. When paired with positive habits, self-discipline becomes a powerful tool that drives success. Imagine the impact on your life when you form habits that are aligned with your values, goals, and dreams.

In earlier weeks, we learned about the importance of:

- **Mindset**: Your thoughts shape your reality.
- **Gratitude and Affirmations**: Shifting your mindset to abundance and positivity.
- **Goal-Setting**: Defining clear, actionable goals.
- **Self-Love and Mental Health**: Taking care of your mental well-being as the foundation for everything else.

Now, let's use all that knowledge to create a routine that aligns with your goals and builds lasting, powerful habits. The key here is consistency.

Step 1: Start with Your Why

Before diving into your routine, remind yourself why you're doing this. What are your big goals? What is your vision for your life? Whether it's excelling in your studies, landing your dream career, or creating lasting relationships, start with clarity about what you want to achieve.

Ask yourself:

- Why do I want to create a perfect routine?
- What is my ultimate goal in life?
- How will my routine support me in achieving that goal?

This will give you direction and help you stay motivated when life gets challenging.

Step 2: Design Your Morning Routine

Your morning routine is the foundation of your day. It sets the tone for everything that follows, so let's make it count! Incorporate elements from previous chapters to create a routine that energizes you, boosts your focus, and prepares you for the day ahead.

Consider including the following activities:

- **Mindful Wake-Up**: Start your day by acknowledging gratitude for waking up and the opportunities ahead.
- **Meditation or Deep Breathing**: A 5-minute meditation session helps calm your mind and sets a peaceful tone for the day. You could also try a few deep breathing exercises.
- **Affirmations and Visualization**: Affirm your goals and envision yourself achieving them. This activates the law of attraction and brings clarity.
- **Exercise**: Whether it's a short stretch or a full workout, movement energizes your body and mind.
- **Healthy Breakfast**: Fuel yourself with a nutritious meal that powers you for the day ahead.

Activity 1: Create Your Ideal Morning Routine

1. Write down the activities you would like to include in your morning routine. Think about the habits from previous chapters (e.g., gratitude, affirmations, meditation).

2. Choose 3 habits to start with. Keep them simple and achievable.

3. Set a goal to practice this routine for the next 7 days. Track your progress and make any adjustments if needed.

Step 3: Time Blocking for Maximum Focus

One of the most powerful strategies for effective time management is time blocking. This is where you allocate specific blocks of time for certain tasks or activities, ensuring that you stay focused and productive.

To apply this to your routine, follow these steps:

- **Prioritize tasks**: Identify your most important tasks for the day and allocate time for them first (e.g., schoolwork, studying, personal projects).
- **Set clear goals for each block:** For example, if you're studying, make sure you know exactly what subjects or chapters you want to focus on during that time.
- **Incorporate breaks:** Remember, regular breaks are essential to prevent burnout. A 5-10 minute break every hour helps maintain focus.

Activity 2: Create Your Time Blocks

1. List your main tasks for the day (e.g., schoolwork, chores, exercise, relaxation).
2. Break them down into blocks. For example: 8 AM to 10 AM – Study Mathematics, 10:30 AM to 11 AM – Break/Walk.
3. Allocate time for breaks and relaxation. Ensure you balance work and rest throughout the day.

Step 4: Practice Mindfulness and Presence

Mindfulness is the practice of being present in the moment without judgment. It's essential for reducing stress, increasing focus, and enhancing your well-being. Integrating mindfulness into your daily routine will help you remain calm and focused, no matter what challenges you face.

Try incorporating these **mindfulness practices:**

- **Mindful eating**: Pay attention to the taste, texture, and aroma of your food during meals.
- **Mindful walking**: While walking, be fully present, noticing the sights, sounds, and sensations around you.
- **Mindful breaks**: Take a few moments during your breaks to simply breathe deeply and release any tension.

Activity 3: Mindfulness Check-In

1. **Pick 2 activities during the day where you can practice mindfulness** (e.g., during breakfast or while walking).
2. **Focus on the present moment**: Take a few deep breaths, notice your surroundings, and pay full attention to what you are doing.
3. **Reflect**: After your mindfulness practice, take a moment to reflect on how you feel. Are you more relaxed? Focused?

Step 5: Evening Routine for Reflection and Recharging

A peaceful and intentional evening routine helps you wind down, reflect on the day, and prepare for tomorrow. It's also essential for improving your sleep quality.

Consider these practices for your evening routine:

- **Reflect on your day**: What went well? What could you improve? Journaling your thoughts will help you reflect on your growth.
- **Set goals for tomorrow**: Write down 2-3 tasks you want to achieve the next day.
- **Relaxation:** Read, practice deep breathing, or listen to calming music. Avoid screens and give yourself time to unwind.
- **Sleep**: Ensure you get enough rest (7-8 hours) to recharge for the next day.

Activity 4: Plan Your Evening Reflection

1. Write down 2-3 things that went well today.
2. Identify 1 thing you want to improve for tomorrow.
3. Create a bedtime routine that promotes relaxation. For example, try reading for 15 minutes before sleep.

Key Takeaways:

- Self-discipline and building positive habits are essential for success and personal growth.
- A structured routine sets the tone for a productive and fulfilling day.
- Morning and evening routines are crucial for energizing, reflecting, and recharging.
- Time blocking ensures you stay focused on what matters most.
- Mindfulness helps you reduce stress and stay present, boosting your overall well-being.
- Regular reflection on your routine helps you track progress and make adjustments.

Conclusion:

Now that you have a clear structure for creating your perfect daily routine, it's time to take action. Start small, be consistent, and adjust your routine as needed. As you build these habits, you will begin to see positive changes in your life.

Remember, this is YOUR journey. You are in control of your time and your success. By following this plan, you'll not only develop the self-discipline needed to reach your goals but also cultivate habits that will set you up for a fulfilling and purposeful life.

Let's create a routine that makes you unstoppable!

XII
Week 12-The Power of Action:Making Your Dream Come True

Dreams are powerful—they inspire, fuel passion, and spark creativity. But dreams alone won't get you where you want to go. **Action is the bridge between where you are now and where you want to be.** In the previous chapters, we've discussed mindset, goal-setting, self-love, and the importance of routines. Now, it's time to take the most critical step: ACT.

In this week, we're going to show you how to make your dreams come true by taking consistent, purposeful action. No more waiting for the "perfect moment" or hoping things will magically fall into place. It's time to step into your potential, and with each action you take, you'll draw closer to your goals.

Why Action is the Key to Success

Have you ever had a dream, set a goal, or visualized a future but found yourself not moving toward it? Why? Often, it's because we get caught up in thinking, planning, or worrying, but we forget to act.

Action is like planting seeds in a garden. If you plant the seeds and nurture them, they will eventually grow. But if you do nothing, those seeds will never sprout. Similarly, you may have a great vision, but without consistent action, that vision will remain just a dream.

Here's the truth: Nothing happens until you take action. Whether it's a small step or a giant leap, each action you take brings you closer to your ultimate goal.

Step 1: Take One Small Step Forward

If your goals feel overwhelming, don't worry. Big dreams are achieved one step at a time. You don't have to climb the whole mountain in one go—just take one small step today. This can be something as simple as reading a chapter of a book that inspires you or making one phone call that moves your project forward.

When you take action, even in small amounts, you create momentum. Every time you act, you get closer to your ultimate goal.

Activity 1: Small Action Step

1. Identify one small task that you can do today to move closer to your dream. It could be related to your studies, your personal development, or even a side project.
2. Take action: Do that task right now, without waiting for the "perfect" moment.
3. Reflect on how it feels. How did taking action make you feel? Write it down.

Step 2: Consistency Is Key

Taking action isn't a one-time event—it's a habit. You have learned the power of routine and consistency in previous weeks. Consistent action, no matter how small, compounds over time. Think about it like this: If you practice a skill every day, you'll get better at it. If you study a little bit every day, you'll become more knowledgeable. Consistency is your secret weapon to success.

Activity 2: Commit to Consistency

1. Write down one action you can take every day that will bring you closer to your goal. This could be studying for 30 minutes, practicing a skill, or learning something new.

2. Commit to doing this action daily for 7 days. Remember, consistency is what builds momentum.
3. Track your progress by writing down your thoughts each day. Celebrate your consistency.

Step 3: Push Through Fear and Doubt

Fear and doubt are natural. In fact, they're often signs that you're stepping out of your comfort zone and moving toward growth. But you don't have to let fear stop you. The best way to overcome fear is by acting anyway. The more you act, the less power fear has over you.

Remember: You don't have to be perfect to start; you just need to start.

Activity 3: Overcoming Fear

1. Identify a fear or doubt that's holding you back from taking action.
2. Write down one small action you can take right now that will push through this fear.
3. Do that action today, even if it's uncomfortable. Reflect on how it feels to take action despite fear.

Step 4: Hold Yourself Accountable

Accountability is powerful. When you tell someone about your goals, it creates a sense of responsibility. You don't have to do this alone. Having someone you trust to check in with can keep you on track and motivated. Whether it's a mentor, a friend, or a family member, accountability can increase your chances of success.

Activity 4: Accountability Partner

1. Choose an accountability partner—someone who will support and encourage you in your journey.
2. Share your goal with them and set a time for regular check-ins.
3. Review your progress together during each check-in.

Step 5: Act with Passion and Purpose

Action should never feel like a chore. It's about tapping into your passion, finding joy in the process, and aligning your actions with your purpose. When you feel inspired by what you're doing, it becomes much easier to take action. Passion fuels persistence.

Activity 5: Connect with Your Passion

1. Write down your passions—the things that excite and inspire you.
2. Reflect on how you can connect your passion with your goals. How can your daily actions bring you closer to your passion?
3. Take one step today that is aligned with your passion and purpose.

Reflecting on What You've Learned

Now that we've covered the importance of action and how to take meaningful steps toward your dreams, let's reflect on everything we've learned throughout this journey:

1. You've learned about the power of mindset, goal-setting, and how to visualize your dreams. But remember: none of this is useful without action.
2. Action is the missing piece. It's the driving force that turns your dreams into reality. Every single step you take, no matter how small, is part of your journey.
3. Taking action requires consistency, overcoming fear, accountability, and connecting with your passion. But most importantly, it requires you to start today.

Key Takeaways

- Action turns dreams into reality. It's the key ingredient that brings everything together.
- Small, consistent steps create momentum. Start with one action today, and build from there.

- Fear is natural—but don't let it stop you. Act anyway, and you'll gain confidence.
- Accountability helps keep you motivated and on track.
- Passion and purpose should guide your actions, making the process enjoyable and meaningful.

Conclusion

Now, it's time for you to act. Your dreams are waiting, and the only thing standing between you and your goals is the action you take. Remember, every single day is an opportunity to move closer to your dream. You've learned the tools, built the mindset, and understood the process. Now, go out there and take action—because **the world is waiting to see you achieve your greatness.**

Conclusion

As we reach the end of this journey together, take a moment to reflect on how far you've come. These past 12 weeks were not just about reading a book; they were about discovering yourself, challenging old beliefs, and creating a roadmap for the life you truly deserve.

You've explored your inner world, identified your strengths, and faced your fears. You've learned to master your time, build healthy relationships, and prioritize your wellness. You've set meaningful goals, embraced self-discipline, and taken action to turn your dreams into reality.

But remember, this journey doesn't end here. The tools, insights, and strategies you've gained are seeds planted in your life. They require nurturing, practice, and perseverance to grow.

Life is not a straight path; it's a journey of continuous learning and evolution. There will be challenges, setbacks, and moments of doubt. But now, you have the mindset and the confidence to face them. You've seen the power of action, the strength in self-awareness, and the joy of living with purpose.

As you step forward, carry these lessons with you:

- Believe in yourself.
- Take small, consistent steps toward your dreams.
- Embrace challenges as opportunities for growth.
- Be kind to yourself and others.

Most importantly, never stop designing the life you deserve. You have the power within you to create a life that is fulfilling, purposeful, and uniquely yours.

This book was just the beginning. Your journey is yours to continue, and I am cheering for you every step of the way.

With gratitude and encouragement,
Simble
+918281556616

About The Author

Simble is a passionate life coach, consultant psychologist, and educator with a deep commitment to empowering others to lead fulfilling, meaningful lives. With a background in engineering and a Master's degree in Psychology, Simble made a courageous career transition to life coaching, drawing on a diverse range of experiences to help individuals unlock their full potential.

Simble began their professional journey at Federal Bank as a trainee before transitioning to academia, where they worked as an Assistant Professor in an engineering college. These early experiences in both the corporate and educational sectors have provided Simble with a comprehensive perspective on personal and professional growth.

As the founder of Life Architects Hub, Simble has successfully guided many students and professionals in overcoming challenges, building self-confidence, and achieving personal and career goals. With a focus on self-love, mental health, productivity, and personal growth, Simble's coaching empowers individuals to discover their true purpose and create lasting change in their lives.

Simble is the author of two paperbacks and three Kindle books, offering deep insights on life coaching, personal development, and mental well-being. In addition, Simble runs a YouTube channel that inspires and educates audiences on how to lead purposeful, fulfilling lives.

Through personalized coaching sessions, engaging content, and a holistic approach to life development, Simble continues to inspire clients from around the world to take charge of their lives, heal past wounds, and create the future they truly deserve.

Driven by a passion for helping others grow, Simble believes that everyone has the power to design their own life and achieve their dreams. In their free time, Simble enjoys reading, writing, and reflecting on new ways to uplift others, leaving a lasting impact on those seeking positive transformation.

For coaching inquiries or support, you can reach Simble at:
Mobile:+91 8281556616
Email:simble.connect@gmail.com

www.ingramcontent.com/pod-product-compliance
Lightning Source LLC
Chambersburg PA
CBHW020642160726
47991CB00003B/991